THE
HURON CAROL

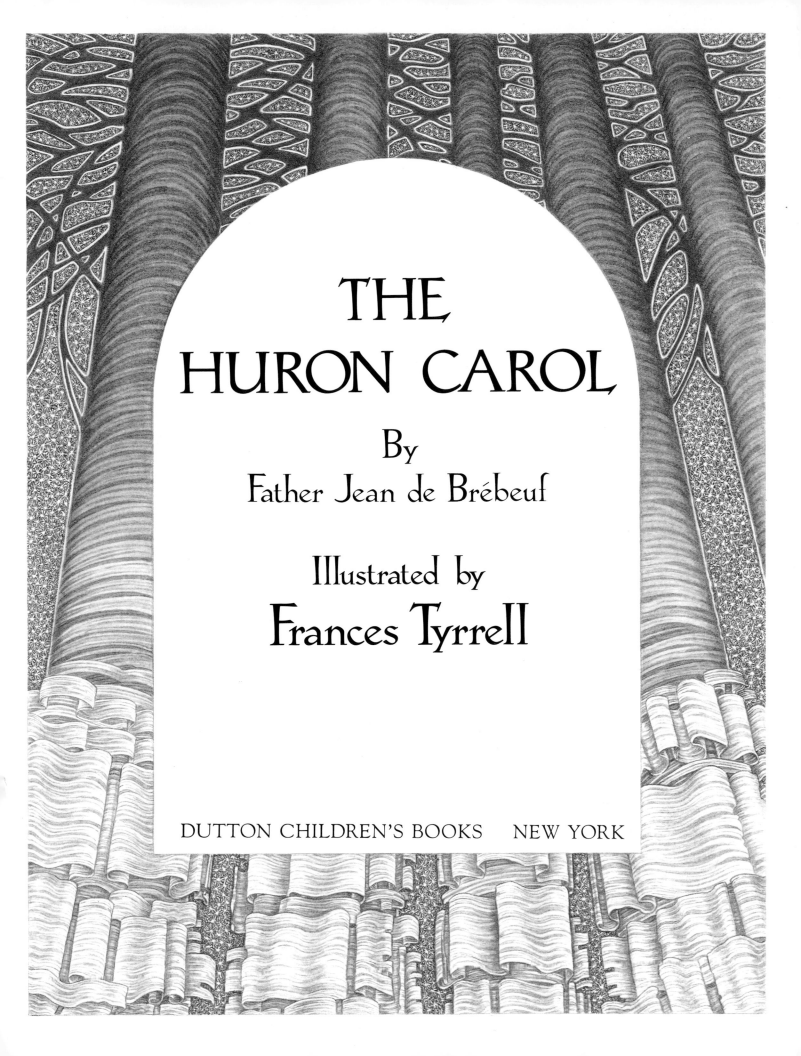

THE
HURON CAROL

By
Father Jean de Brébeuf

Illustrated by
Frances Tyrrell

DUTTON CHILDREN'S BOOKS   NEW YORK

Illustrations copyright © 1990 by Frances Tyrrell
English text copyright © 1926 by J. E. Middleton

All rights reserved.
English words reprinted with the kind permission of
The Frederick Harris Music Co., Limited

CIP Data is available.

First published in the United States by Dutton Children's Books
a division of Penguin Books USA Inc.
375 Hudson Street, New York, New York 10014

Originally published in Canada 1990 by Lester & Orpen Dennys Limited

Printed in Hong Kong
First U.S. Edition N 10 9 8 7 6 5 4 3 2 1

ISBN 0-525-44909-4

for my parents, Avril and Don

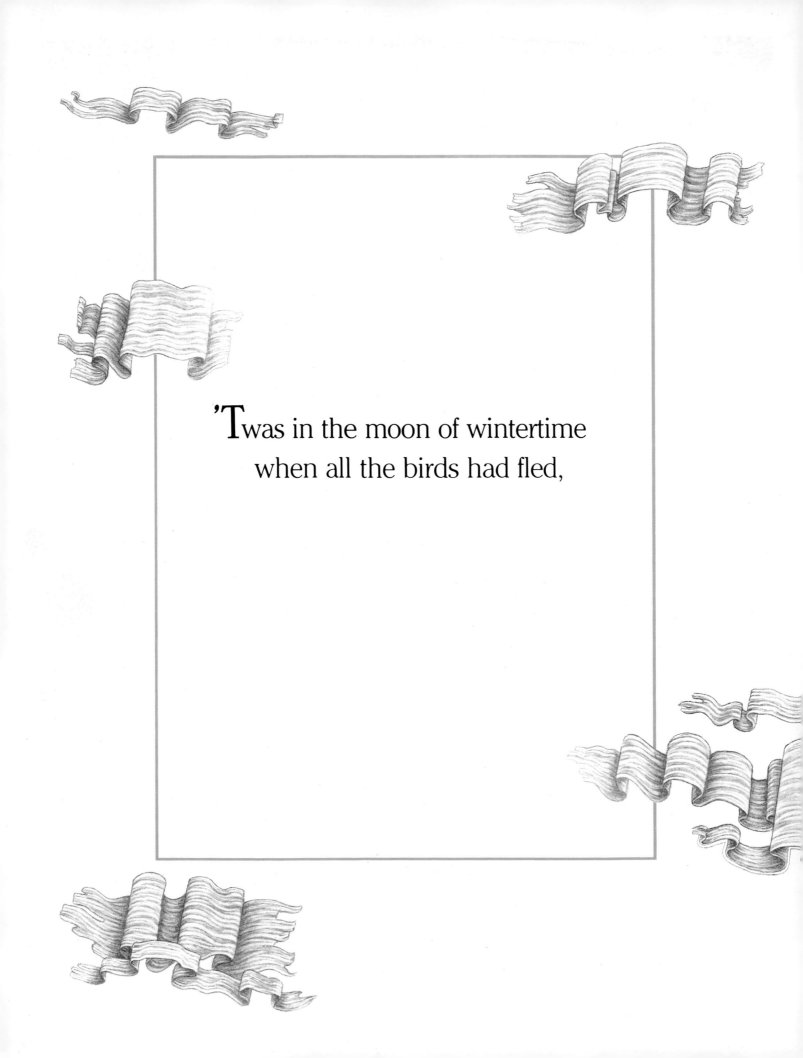

'Twas in the moon of wintertime
when all the birds had fled,

That mighty Gitchi Manitou
sent angel choirs instead;

Before their light
the stars grew dim
And wond'ring hunters
heard the hymn:

"Jesus your King is born,
Jesus is born.
In excelsis gloria!"

Within a lodge of broken bark
the tender Babe was found,
A ragged robe of rabbit skin
enwrapped His beauty 'round;

And as the hunter
braves drew nigh,
The angel song
rang loud and high:

"Jesus your King is born,
Jesus is born.
In excelsis gloria!"

The earliest moon of wintertime
is not so round and fair
As was the ring of glory
on the helpless Infant there.

The chiefs from far
before Him knelt
With gifts of fox
and beaver pelt.

"Jesus your King is born,
Jesus is born.
In excelsis gloria!"

O children of the forest free,
O sons of Manitou,
The Holy Child of earth and heaven
is born today for you.

Come kneel before
the radiant Boy
Who brings you beauty,
peace and joy.

"Jesus your King is born,
Jesus is born.
In excelsis gloria!"

1. 'Twas in the moon of win - ter - time When
1. Chré - tiens, pre - nez cou - ra - - ge, Jé -
1. Es - ten - nia - lon de tson - ou - e Je -

all the birds had fled, That might - y Git - chi Man - i - tou sent
sus Sau - veur est ne! Du mat - in les ou - vra - ges A
sous a - ha - ton - hia, On - naou - a - te - ou - a d'o - ki N'on -

an - gel choirs in - stead; Be - fore their light the stars grew dim and
ja - mais sont rui - nés; Quand il chan - te mer - veil - le, A
ouan - da - skoua - en - tak; En - non - chien skou - a - tri - ho - tat, N'on -

won - d'ring hunt - ers heard the hymn:_ "Je - sus your King is born,
ces trou - blants ap - pas, _____ Ne pre - tez plus l'or - eille:
ou - an - di - lon - ra - cha - tha, ___ Je - sous a - ha - ton - hia,

Je - sus is born: In ex - cel - sis glo - ri - a!"
"Jé - sus est né: In ex - cel - sis glo - ri - a!"
Je - - sous a - ha - ton - hi - a!

2. Within a lodge of broken bark
   The tender Babe was found.
   A ragged robe of rabbit skin
   Enwrapped His beauty 'round;
   And as the hunter braves drew nigh
   The angel song rang loud and high:
      "Jesus, your King, is born,
       Jesus is born: In excelsis gloria!"

3. The earliest moon of wintertime
   Is not so round and fair
   As was the ring of glory
   On the helpless Infant there.
   The chiefs from far before him knelt
   With gifts of fox, and beaver pelt.
      "Jesus, your King, is born,
       Jesus is born: In excelsis gloria!"

4. O children of the forest free,
   O sons of Manitou,
   The Holy Child of earth and heaven
   Is born today for you.
   Come kneel before the radiant Boy
   Who brings you beauty, peace, and joy.
      "Jesus, your King, is born,
       Jesus is born: In excelsis gloria!"

2. Oyez cette nouvelle,
   Oont un ange est porteur!
   Oyez! âmes fidèles,
   Et dilatez vos coeurs.
   La Vièrge dans l'étable
   Entours de ses bras
   L'Enfant-Dieu adorable.
      "Jésus est né: In excelsis gloria!"

We have found only one surviving verse in the old Huron language, and two verses in eighteenth-century French, very different from that used today. Enjoy singing the carol in each language.

The Story of the Huron Carol

Many of the Christian Missionaries who came to the New World did not understand that the native peoples already had religions of their own. The Huron Carol is unusual for its time because its composer, the Jesuit missionary Father Jean de Brébeuf, recognized the strength of the Huron beliefs.

Father Jean de Brébeuf (1593-1649) worked among the Huron Indians in the villages around Fort Ste Marie, where Midland, Ontario now stands. During his twenty-two years there he translated many books into the Huron language. But he is best remembered for this telling of the Christmas story in the setting of the Hurons.

Father Jean de Brébeuf was killed after an Iroquois raid. The Iroquois forced the Hurons from their homes. Some went west, some south to what is now Oklahoma. Others followed the Jesuits to Quebec. But the Huron people continued to sing the carol. It was sung in the Huron language for one hundred years, then translated into French, and then into English by J. E. Middleton in 1926. Frances Tyrrell, the illustrator of this book, has tried to make each picture accurate. For instance, the constellations that appear in the borders are those which would have been in a December sky in 1648. The chiefs who come from afar are wearing the clothing of the Kootenay from the Pacific coast, the Sioux from the Plains and the Shawnee from the Woodlands. The palisades and the longhouses look like those that would have surrounded Fort Ste Marie when Father Jean de Brébeuf lived there.

Lack of respect for other people's beliefs has brought much heartache and suffering. But the Huron carol deserves to be remembered and enjoyed because it touches something in all of us: its message–that even in the darkest winter there is the promise of light and new birth–is one of hope which we all can share.

The Grand Chief of the Huron-Wendate Nation, Max Gros-Louis, writes, "Today there are over 2,000 people living on our reserve at the heart of Quebec City. This Nation is a dynamic one. We operate schools, a bank, a radio station, and our own justice system. We are pleased that this book tells a part of our common history."